CAMBRIDGE
CHRISTIAN H

• The Benedictines •

'The monks are to bear with patience the weaknesses of others, whether of body or behaviour. Let them strive with each other in obedience to each other. Let them not follow their own good, but the good of others. Let them be charitable towards their brothers with pure affection.'

RULE OF ST BENEDICT

St Bene't's, which is dedicated to St Benedict and bears the saint's name, albeit in a contracted form, is the oldest church in Cambridge, dating back to Saxon times, *c.*1025. The tower was built during the reign of King Canute and some portions of the original nave still remain. Today the church is cared for by Anglican Franciscan friars. The neighbouring college of Corpus Christi, founded in 1352, used St Bene't's as its chapel until the 16th century and the Parker Library in the college contains a priceless collection of Anglo-Saxon and medieval manuscripts. The most ancient of these are the Canterbury Gospels. These were brought to Canterbury in 597 by Augustine and his fellow Benedictine monks as part of Pope Gregory's mission to the English.

Below: *Above the restored Saxon arch in St Bene't's Church is a stained-glass window depicting St Benedict.*

Below: *The long and short corner-stones of the tower of St Bene't's are typically Saxon. Above the double belfry windows are circular openings, probably to allow owls to enter and prey on the church mice.*

St Benedict (*c.*480–547), whose Rule has made him the father of monasticism in western Europe, was one of the most influential Christian pioneers. The order which he founded at Monte Cassino, near Naples, Italy, in *c.*529, grew rapidly, due largely to the encouragement of Pope Gregory the Great. Benedict's Rule made a unique contribution to European civilisation throughout the Middle Ages and he had a deep influence on Pope Gregory, who wrote the saint's biography. The Benedictine monks became noted for both their scholarship and Gregorian plainsong. In 1964, Benedict was declared patron saint of all Europe by Pope Paul VI.

• The Crusaders •

'... to Randolf with the Beard of Cambridge, to Robert, to Auger and the others of the Fraternity of the Holy Sepulchre, the churchyard of St George and the neighbouring land for construction of a church there in honour of the Holy Sepulchre.'

CHRONICLES OF RAMSEY ABBEY

The original Church of the Holy Sepulchre, known as the Church of the Resurrection, was consecrated in Jerusalem in 335, over the traditional site where Jesus rose from the dead. It was round so that pilgrims could walk around the site of the empty tomb of Jesus. The church in Cambridge, now commonly known as the Round Church, was built *c.*1130, after the first Crusade. The earliest reference to it, from a charter granted by Reinald, Abbot of Ramsey, is quoted above. The 'Fraternity' preceded the Knights Templar and the charter may date back to as early as 1114.

This building is a fine example of Norman architecture, although there have been many additions over the centuries. Much of the Norman work was rebuilt by the Camden Society, who played a major part in the church's restoration. The restored church was re-dedicated in 1843, in the presence of Queen Victoria and Prince Albert.

Since 1994, when the growing congregation moved to the church of St Andrew the Great, the Round Church has become the centre for Cambridge Christian Heritage.

It is likely that the church began as a wayside oratory where people could offer prayers for those connected with the Crusades. Today, prayers are said regularly for reconciliation and peace throughout the world.

Left: *Eight massive Norman pillars with individually carved heads support the vaulted roof of the circular aisle in the Round Church. Some of the stone diagonals are carved in the distinctive dog-tooth pattern of the period.*

• Royal Piety •

'O Lord Jesus Christ, who hast created and redeemed me, and hast brought me unto that which now I am; thou knowest what thou wouldest do with me; do with me according to thy will, for thy tender mercy's sake.'

HENRY VI'S PRAYER, BASED ON LUKE 1:38

Before he was 20 years old, Henry VI (1421–71) had started two great projects which absorbed his interest for much of his life and have survived until the present day: he founded Eton College in 1440 and King's College a year later. About the teachers he said: '*I would rather have them somewhat weak in music than defective in knowledge of Scripture.*' The chapel of King's, the last and finest Gothic building to be erected in Europe, was his greatest achievement, although he did not live to see its completion.

A very devout man, Henry was generous to the poor, hated cruelty and immorality, and spent many hours each week in meditation and prayer. Temperamentally unsuited to many of his royal duties, he lost the empire that his father Henry V had won in France. In the eyes of his contemporaries, Henry was guilty of an unforgivable sin for a king: like Christ, he forgave those who tried to murder him rather than execute them! His words in the Tower of London, spoken shortly before he was murdered, summed up his life: '*The kingdom of heaven, unto which I have devoted myself always from a child, do I call and cry for. For this kingdom which is transitory and of the earth I do not greatly care.*'

Right: *The bronze lectern in the chapel at King's College is surmounted by a statue of the founder, Henry VI. The lectern holds the Old and New Testaments, the latter surrounded by emblems of the four Evangelists. Both are guarded by lions at the base.*

Below: *King's College chapel (left) was founded by Henry VI in 1446. Above the archway in the adjacent 18th-century façade, the work of Gibbs, is a semi-circular window. This opens onto the drawing-room where Charles Simeon, the great evangelical leader, held his famous classes for undergraduates.*

• The New Learning •

'I wish that the Scriptures might be translated into all languages, so that not only the Scots and Irish, but also the Turk and the Saracen might read and understand them. I long that the farm-labourer might sing them as he follows his plough, the weaver hum them to the tune of his shuttle, and the traveller beguile the weariness of his journey with their stories.'

ERASMUS

One of the University's great benefactors was Lady Margaret Beaufort (1443–1509), wife of Edmund Tudor, mother of Henry VII and the founder of the Tudor dynasty. Persuaded by her chaplain, John Fisher, she endowed a Chair of Divinity and founded the colleges of Christ's and St John's.

Fisher (1469–1535) became the first Lady Margaret Professor of Divinity. An ardent promoter of the 'New Learning' of the Renaissance, he advocated radical moral reform within the Church. After refusing to recognise Henry VIII as head of the Church of England he was beheaded on Tower Hill, London. As he walked to his execution, he read aloud: '*This is life eternal that they might know thee the only true God, and Jesus Christ, whom thou hast sent*' (John 17:3). He was canonised in 1935.

The Dutch humanist and scholar Erasmus (*c.*1466–1536) was the most illustrious of many prominent thinkers invited to Cambridge by Fisher. He succeeded Fisher as Professor of Divinity and was also Professor of Greek. His edition of the New Testament, with parallel Greek and Latin texts, which was published in 1516, 'laid the egg' that was to be hatched by the Reformers.

***Left:** The statues flanking the entrance to St John's College chapel are of John Fisher and Lady Margaret Beaufort, treading under foot the symbols of vice and ignorance.*

***Above:** Born in Rotterdam, Desiderius Erasmus was one of the most influential of the Renaissance scholars. Widely travelled, he studied and taught in most of the great cultural centres of Europe.*

• The Reformers •

'By his confession I learned more than before in many years. So from that time forward I began to smell the Word of God and forsook the school doctors and such fooleries.'

LATIMER, OF BILNEY

St Edward's is justifiably called 'The Cradle of the English Reformation' because it was here that Cambridge nurtured the leaders of this movement. Although the works of Luther were burned outside the west door of Great St Mary's in 1521, they continued to be discussed in the White Horse Inn (next to King's) and the Reformers began to preach their new-found doctrines at St Edward's, exposing the worldliness of the Catholic Church.

Thomas Bilney (*c.*1495–1531), of Trinity Hall, was one of the first of these leaders. He was imprisoned in the Tower of London for his fearless preaching of Justification by Faith, prior to being burned in the Lollards' Pit at Norwich. Hugh Latimer (*c.*1485–1555), Fellow of Clare College and a gifted preacher, who was persuaded of the truth of this doctrine by Bilney, eventually suffered the same fate at Oxford. With him died Nicholas Ridley (*c.*1500–1555), another ardent and outspoken Reformer, and Master of Pembroke College, who assisted Thomas Cranmer in preparing the Thirty-Nine Articles. Bilney, Latimer and Robert Barnes, Prior of the nearby Augustinian friary, are commemorated within the walls of St Edward's.

St Mary the Great, the University church, has always been famous for its preachers, of whom Cranmer (1489–1556), the first Protestant Archbishop of Canterbury, was one. He wrote the magnificent preface to the Great Bible of 1540, which was placed in every church in England. With Ridley and the German Protestant Reformer Martin Bucer, he prepared the 1552 Prayer Book, which became the basis of the 1662 Book of Common Prayer. Cranmer annulled Henry VIII's marriage to Catherine of Aragon and supported the Act of Supremacy, which proclaimed the sovereign as head of the Church of England. In 1556, in Oxford, he was burned as a heretic for rejecting the Catholic faith.

Bucer (1491–1551), who had been invited to Cambridge by Cranmer in 1549 as Regius Professor of Theology, had worked hard to reconcile Catholics and Protestants in Germany. He was buried in Great St Mary's but, in 1557, on the orders of Mary Tudor, his coffin was exhumed and burned in the market-place. A brass plate in the chancel of

Left: *The Church of St Edward King and Martyr is dedicated to a little-known Saxon king of England, who was murdered in 979. It has close associations with the early Reformers, many of whom are commemorated within its walls.*

Left: St Mary the Great, with its distinctive late Perpendicular Gothic lines, is the principal church in the city and most of the Cambridge Reformers preached here. A plaque near the altar shows where Bucer was buried.

• TUDOR MONARCHS •	
Henry VII	1485–1509
Henry VIII	1509–1547
Edward VI	1547–1553
Mary I	1553–1558
Elizabeth I	1558–1603

St Mary's records that a second memorial service was held during the reign of Elizabeth I. Bucer is now remembered as the 'Father of Calvinism'.

Thomas Cartwright (1535–1603), who was appointed Lady Margaret Professor of Divinity during the reign of Elizabeth I, was a fervent Puritan. His powerful nonconformist lectures filled St Mary's to overflowing and the verger had to remove some of the windows so that the crowds outside could hear him. In 1570, he lectured in the church on the book of Acts, which he claimed supported the Presbyterian form of church government. As a result of this he was relieved of his professorship and exiled from Cambridge. He later became known as the 'Father of English Presbyterianism'.

Below: *This plaque in St Edward's commemorates Thomas Bilney, Robert Barnes (Prior of the Augustinian monastery in Cambridge) and Hugh Latimer, all of whom were burned at the stake.*

Right: *Hugh Latimer preached from this 16th-century oak pulpit. Lost for a time, it was returned to St Edward's in 1949 when the Latimer memorial window was installed.*

• The Puritans •

'It should be a seed-plot of learned men for the supply of the Church, and for the sending forth of as large a number as possible of those who shall instruct the people in the Christian faith.'

SIR WALTER MILDMAY'S PLAN FOR EMMANUEL COLLEGE

Emmanuel College was founded by Sir Walter Mildmay, Chancellor of the Exchequer to Elizabeth I, in 1584. It was built on the site of a Dominican friary which Henry VIII had dissolved in 1538. The college quickly became the centre of Protestant theology in Cambridge.

Thirty-five of the early settlers who emigrated to the New World in the 17th century, to escape religious persecution, were Emmanuel graduates. John Harvard (1607–38), the best known, sailed for Charleston, Massachusetts, in 1637. Sadly, he died within a year of arriving but he bequeathed half his estate and over 300 books to a newly founded college (1636) at Cambridge, Massachusetts. This college later became Harvard University, the oldest and one of the most famous of the universities in the United States.

John Harvard is commemorated in one of the Emmanuel chapel windows. He is depicted bearing a scroll with the following inscription, in Latin: '*The people which shall be created shall praise the Lord*' (Psalm 102:18).

Above: *John Harvard, one of the early settlers, is depicted in this window of Emmanuel chapel with an urn labelled* Sal Gentium *(Salt of the Nations).*

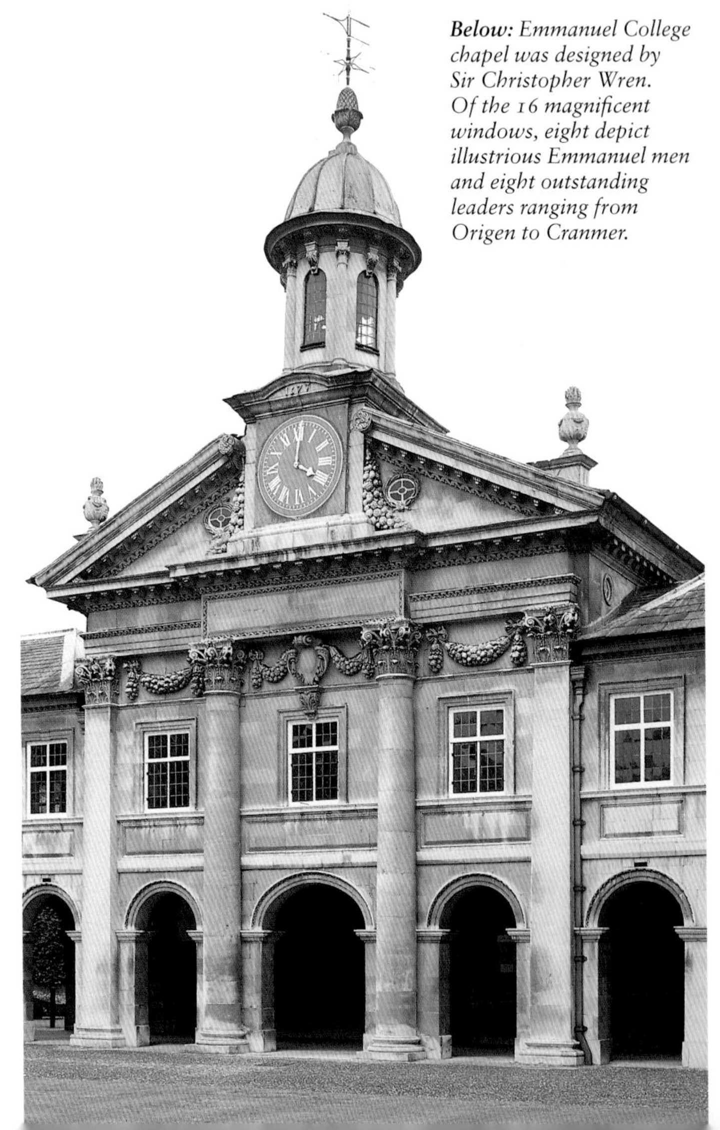

Below: *Emmanuel College chapel was designed by Sir Christopher Wren. Of the 16 magnificent windows, eight depict illustrious Emmanuel men and eight outstanding leaders ranging from Origen to Cranmer.*

• Science and Humanity •

'This most beautiful system of the sun, planets and comets, could only proceed from the counsel and dominion of an intelligent and powerful Being.'

ISAAC NEWTON, PHILOSOPHIAE NATURALIS PRINCIPIA MATHEMATICA

***Right:** During his time at Trinity, Isaac Newton occupied the first-floor room just to the right of the College gate. It was here that he wrote his* Principia Mathematica.

Trinity College's most outstanding scientist and mathematician was Isaac Newton (1642–1727). Apart from his revolutionary work on gravitation, published in *Philosophiae Naturalis Principia Mathematica* in 1687, he was also well known for his studies on differential calculus and the nature of light. Newton became Lucasian Professor of Mathematics when just 27 years old, a post he was to hold for the next 33 years. A student of alchemy, he also wrote a history of Creation and a remarkable commentary on the book of Daniel and on the Apocalypse. His statue stands in the ante-chapel of Trinity.

The philanthropist William Wilberforce (1759–1833) was educated at St John's College and was converted to evangelical Christianity during a tour of the Continent. In 1788, supported by the Quakers and Thomas Clarkson, also of St John's, he began his 40-year struggle in the House of Commons which culminated in the abolition of the slave trade (1807) and of slavery (1833) in the British Empire. '*Never, never will we desist till we have wiped away this scandal from the Christian name, released ourselves from the load of guilt under which we at present labour, and extinguished every trace of this bloody traffic of which our posterity, looking back to the history of these enlightened times, will scarce believe that it has been suffered to exist so long a disgrace and dishonour to this country.*'

***Right:** This statue of William Wilberforce, best known for his fight to abolish the slave trade, stands in the chapel of St John's College.*

• Missionaries and Preachers •

'The sort of men who are wanted for missionaries are such as I see before me – men of education, zeal and piety.'

DAVID LIVINGSTONE, SPEECH IN THE SENATE HOUSE, 1857

Right: *The original Holy Trinity Church was destroyed by fire in the 12th century. The present building is the product of several periods of development.*

Below: *Charles Simeon ministered in Holy Trinity for 54 years. A number of his possessions are housed in the vestry, including a teapot and a large green umbrella – probably the first umbrella ever seen in Cambridge!*

In the latter half of the 18th century, Holy Trinity Church became the centre of evangelical Christianity in Cambridge and several outstanding people are celebrated within its walls. Charles Simeon (1759–1836), a renowned preacher, a Fellow of King's College and leader of the evangelical revival of the Church of England, was vicar here from 1782 until his death. In the pulpit his declared aim was '*to humble the sinner, exalt the Saviour, and promote holiness*'; outside the pulpit, he instructed students in theology and taught them to expound the scriptures. However, his influence ranged far more widely than Cambridge. The mission field was a cause he held dear and he was instrumental in forming the Church Missionary Society in 1793, to which no less than 140 students were to offer their services between 1873 and 1889. He was also associated with the formation of the British and Foreign Bible Society. There is a handsome memorial to Simeon in the chancel, bearing his chosen epitaph: '*I determined to know nothing except Jesus Christ and Him crucified*' (1 Corinthians 2:2).

Henry Martyn (1781–1812) was one of Simeon's converts. Martyn graduated from St John's in 1801 and became a Fellow the following year. He then sailed for India in 1805, as a chaplain with the East India Company. A self-taught linguist, he translated the New Testament into Hindustani (Urdu), Persian